NYC
8/23/2023

BEST
OF LUCK!!

MW01034358

"Welcome to Ron Kolm's world, a world of many bookstores and chance encounters. Jump into these pages and rub shoulders with literary luminaries and celebrities like Philip Roth, Jerry Brown, William Kunstler, Charles Bukowski, Valerie Solanas and punk rockers Tom Verlaine and Patti Smith, both of whom the author shelved books with in the Strand Bookstore. Beyond brushes with celebrities, there are weird moments he recounts in abundance. How to handle a junkie nodding out without getting books knocked off the shelves, or dealing with a panic-stricken store evacuation after a Con Ed steampipe has exploded a couple of blocks away, shooting debris high into the surrounding sky. This is Ron Kolm's world, and his signature dead-pan delivery is in fine form in this book." --George Wallace, writer in residence, Walt Whitman Birthplace.

"Ron Kolm's new book is an ode to an era, to the magic of books, to authors he revered and those he worked with or ran into on the job. A brilliant storyteller, Kolm enlightens and entertains readers with crisp, colorful prose and poetry based on interactions with quirky bosses, writers, and customers. With the city's landmark bookstores as backdrop, he writes collages based on relics found in used books and publishes works as a member of the edgy Unbearable Poets. A passionate tribute to the printed page, *The Bookstore book* offers a treasure of stories that will delight readers and fellow bibliophiles." --Amy Barone, author of *Defying Extinction* and *We Became Summer.*

"Ron Kolm's genre defying memoir reads like manna from heaven sure to delight any bibliophile worth their salt. As a poet and writer who reads his work all over the city, we know how Ron spends his nights. Now we know how he spends his days. And what a rich life it is. Populated with a cast of characters you will recognize; the pages of *The Bookstore Book* give us a warm embrace of a vanishing New York. This volume belongs in your hands and then on your shelf; more than an artifact, it is a celebration of the joy and soul-sustaining force provided by sitting down with a really good book." --Danny Shot, author of *WORKS.*

"Here are Ron Kolm's funnaminal records of his fifty-year career of working in New York City's independent bookstores. Ron witnessed the liberal Democratic governor, Jerry Brown, buying Hitler's *Mein Kampf* and chased sexist Ugly George up Broadway. Hilarious. He's cooked up a story about enjoying a late lunch at The Russian Tea Room with Philip Roth's Wiedergänger who is ordering a plateful of *Cotelette à la Kiev*. And he tells us that he couldn't order books because Kathy Acker of *Blood and Guts in High School* fame was talking endlessly on the New Morning Bookstore's phone. *The Bookstore Book* is an exhilarating literary monument to the dying trade of bookselling." --Jürgen Schneider, author of the novel *RMX*, the Vienna diary *Anilingasse* and two books about James Joyce.

"Ron Kolm documents his bibliophile's journey in *The Bookstore Book: A Memoir*. Bookstores are places to meander aisles, searching for treasures of knowledge and gratification on the shelves. We get to meet Allen Ginsberg, William Burroughs, Philip Roth, Joseph Heller's daughter, Erica, and an ancient street icon called Ugly George. Never dull, always an adventure on each page, enticing the reader to ask for more of Kolm's "tales of the city." --Patricia Carragon, author of *Angel Fire* (Alien Buddha Press) and *Meowku* (Poets Wear Prada) is curator/editor-in-chief Brownstone Poets, Brooklyn, NY.

"Ron Kolm's *The Bookstore Book* is a wry tour de force, a clever compendium of insightful stories and anecdotes on art and life in NYC. In poetry and prose the bookstore becomes a microcosm and metaphor for Kolm's life experience. It contains shapely honed anecdotes on celebrity -- those tormented souls we call artists. A roller coaster ride, vivid and insightful." --Dorothy Friedman August is an award-winning poet, editor of *White Rabbit* zine and co-editor of *Downtown Poets*.

"*The Bookstore Book* is a beautifully written tale of a poet's life in New York City." --Chavisa Woods, author of *100 Times (A Memoir of Sexism)*, is also the Executive Director of *A Gathering of the Tribes*.

The Bookstore Book

A Memoir

The Bookstore Book

A Memoir

Ron Kolm

Pink Trees Press
New York City

Titles from Pink Trees Press

Origami Book #1, Linda Kleinbub
Origami Book #2, Linda Kleinbub
Silver Tongued Devil Anthology, Linda Kleinbub &
Anthony C. Murphy, Editors
Poems from an Unending Pandemic, Phillip Giambri
Dysfunction: A Play on Words in the Familiar,
Pauline Findlay
Good Boy, Bad Boy, A Better Man, Phillip Giambri
Naming a Hurricane, Madeline Artenberg
The Bookstore Book, Ron Kolm

For more information email
Pink Trees Press at PinkTreesPress@gmail.com or
Linda Kleinbub at Linda.Kleinbub@gmail.com

DEDICATION

This book is dedicated to my wife, Donna,
and my two sons, Daniel and Gregory.

GRATITUDE

I want to thank Linda Kleinbub, Madeline Artenberg,
Phillip Giambri, and Pink Trees Press for all the
wonderful work they have done for the world of
words! I am so grateful!

I'd also like to thank Jennifer Sy, Jenn Ross and
Andy Owen of Posman Books, George Leibson,
Richard Urciuoli, Mike Lindgren, Jim Boyett,
Floyd Sykes, Ronald Stephenson, Annie Vaccaro and
Richard Klonfas of Coliseum Books, Jim Drougas,
the founder of New Morning Bookstore, Peter Dargis,
Bob Contant, Terry McCoy and Tom Evans of
East Side Bookstore / St. Mark's Bookshop and
Fred Bass, Brian Bailey, Richard Hell and
Patti Smith, who all worked at the Strand Book Store,
and so many other terrific booksellers
I've known down through the years!

I want to thank two editors who will be using some of
my poems on the COVID-19 pandemic in their
anthologies. *Covid Chronicles: The Pandemic in the
Words of New Yorkers,* edited by Robert W. Snyder,
is forthcoming from Cornell University Press. *The
COVID Poetry Files*, edited by Evie Ivy, will be
published by Ra Rays Press.

Some of these pieces previously appeared in
*A Change in the Weather, Flapperhouse, Local
Knowledge, Night Shift, NYC From the Inside,
Poetry Super Highway, Sensitive Skin Magazine,
The Brooklyn Rail, The Café Review, The Opiate*
and *Urban Graffiti Daily.*

Graphics by: Bill Anthony, Bob Eckstein
(from his book *Footnotes from the World's Greatest
Bookstores: True Tales and Lost Moments from Book
Buyers, Booksellers, and Book Lovers*), Dan Freeman,
Jeffrey Isaac, Shalom Neuman and Gregory Kolm.
Cover photograph, 'Posman Books Chelsea Market,'
by Daniel Kolm.

Published in the United States of America by
Pink Trees Press
Middle Village, NY 11379

First Edition May 2023
ISBN: 978-1-66640-206-3
Library of Congress Control Number: 2023908571

Table of Contents

Prose

Interview

Poems

Graphics

PROSE

Encyclopedia Salesman

"We all live in a yellow submarine, yellow submarine, yellow submarine," Lenny sings along with the car radio, as he drives us on the turnpike across central Pennsylvania.

"Hey, Lenny, no one lives in a fucking yellow submarine – that's all bullcrap!" one of the kids, a college student named Rick, shouts from the back seat.

"We all live in a broken-down barn, a burnt-out…" Lenny jokes, looking in the rear-view mirror.

"Hey, keep your eyes on the road – oh shit!"

"Hold on, just blew a tire."

Lenny's battered Chevy station wagon skids across the highway, finally coming to a stop on the shoulder, where we all breathe a sigh of relief.

"That was a close one, man. You almost sunk the submarine, skipper!"

"Aw, pipe down, my lemmings. I'll be right back." Lenny jumps out of the wagon and heads around to the rear, opens it, and flips up the floorboard over the spare tire and emergency jack. He proceeds to use them very efficiently, and in just a couple of minutes we're back on the road, heading towards Mechanicsburg.

We'd left Center City Philadelphia about an hour ago, and Lenny, who is a lot older than us, is our 'boss.' Most of us are still in school – we're doing this gig as a summer job. But Lenny has been living in the real world for quite a while and he's figured out how to cope with it. As he drives, he tells us stories about his adventures: how he had been in the Army, in the quartermaster corps, based in Germany not too long after the end of the war. He and his buddies had run off with everything that was supposed to go to the troops, including Army issue meals, and then sold it at absurdly inflated prices to the locals. Of course, this meant empty cupboards for the G.I.s they were supposed to be supplying with food and fuel. He thought it was funny that American troops had to requisition even the most basic staples from the German population they were billeted among.

Anyway, what Lenny had been hired to do for the company we worked for was to transport us to an obviously poor neighborhood in a post-industrial city a couple of hours from Philly and drop us off in a scattershot pattern, like paratroopers bailing out of a plane behind enemy lines. Our mission was to sell sets of encyclopedias. Lenny would scribble the names of the cross streets on a scrap of paper and tell us 'salesmen' that he would stop back in five hours at that exact location, and the 'salesman' better be there. Or else. We all wore watches – time was not necessarily on our side.

The neighborhoods we were turned loose into had to fit a profile. Lenny would drive until he found the poor part of town; ancient row houses, broken down duplexes, etc., and we would look for battered toys in the front yards – that was important. If there was no evidence of kids around, Lenny would continue to scout around in different areas of the city until he found some.

After getting out of his car, I would take a deep breath to clear my mind as I watched my teammates vanish into the distance. That was my way of getting rid of any ethical considerations that were still knocking around inside me. Then I'd check out my surroundings looking for the nearest house most likely to have a prospective client inside. I looked for peeling paint, exposed sheets of tarpaper under damaged fake brick siding, unmowed lawns, windows with missing panes of glass. After choosing a victim, I would unlatch the front gate, if there was one, and walk up the usually cracked cement walk to the front door and ring the doorbell. If there wasn't a doorbell, I would knock loudly.

Someone usually answered: a haggard young mother with curlers in her hair, an unemployed ex-steelworker -- sometimes it was both parents with their kids -- opening the door a crack and asking what I wanted.

I always followed the script we had been carefully coached to use:

"I would like to help you with some of your problems. May I come in and talk to you? I promise not to take up too much of your time."

And the person, or persons, at the door were invariably nice – deferential to you because you were dressed in slightly better clothes – you had to be careful not to overdress – we had been trained to impress, but not intimidate. And, as you followed them into their home, you continued to follow the script:

"Nice place you have here…Mr…. (or Mrs….)"

"Jones."

Eventually you would end up on a worn sofa, in a dingy living room, light struggling to come in through the dirty windows, facing one or both parents

17

whose children had left the broken toys outside on the lawn, or on the porch.

"So, how can you help us?" you'd be asked. "Well, this is about your kids," you'd answer. "I would guess you'd want them to have a better life than you. Did you graduate from high school, Mr. Jones? Did you Mrs. Jones? No? Wouldn't it be great if your kids did?" And this is where you would try to get the parent, or parents, to agree with you. The word for this procedure is "qualifying" – you would go for as many "yesses" as you could get. And then you came in with the pitch, "Two dimes a day, that's all it would cost, two dimes a day in this tiny cardboard box, and you would soon have enough to buy this wonderful set of encyclopedias that would guarantee that your children would eventually make it through high school, and then go on to college. Just two dimes a day, that's all."

And it usually worked.

###

That Fall I left my parents' house outside of Philadelphia, and went away to college in Reading, Pennsylvania. To help pay for my textbooks and tuition, I got a part-time job in a bookstore. I sold New Directions and City Lights books, which I loved, and even the occasional encyclopedia!

A Philadelphia Story

I worked in a bookstore in Reading, Pennsylvania, when I was in college. It was quite different from a New York City bookstore; we sold furniture, school supplies and an interesting assortment of snacks. I did my best to make the stock we carried respectable; I ordered Joyce, Beckett and Updike, who had lived in Shillington, a suburb of Reading, in his youth. Most of our customers just wanted a fast read. I sympathized but pushed my favorite authors on them anyway. The owner would take me aside and tell me to cut it out. I'd shrug my shoulders and he'd hiss, "Only bums do that."

I didn't like him very much.

There was a lot of dead time; Reading was not a reading city; so I would flip through the art books and look at the color plates to get through the long afternoons. I discovered the Surrealists, and that's when my life changed. I made up my mind that someday I would be part of a circle of writers and artists just like them. And then, by logical extension, I stumbled upon the Dadaists. Marcel Duchamp became my idol – I devoured his works: *The Bride Stripped Bare, Nude Descending a Staircase* and the *Chocolate Grinder*. I read that several of his pieces were in the Philadelphia Museum of Art, in the Arensberg Collection, and that his final work, 'Given: 1. The Waterfall, 2. The Illuminating Gas', a mixed media assemblage consisting of a wooden door surrounded by bricks concealing something, was there, too. But I couldn't find an illustration or description of what was behind it anywhere, so I knew I would have to go to the City of Brotherly Love and check it out in person.

My parents still lived outside of Philly in the house I'd grown up in. I went down to see them and made plans to visit the Museum.

Unfortunately, when I did manage to get there the wing of the Museum with the Arensberg Collection in it was closed to the public due to budget cuts. A fiscal crisis had swept across the nation, and it hit Philadelphia hard. The Museum of Art is like a large U; basically, two wings jutting out from the main building, and they only had enough money to guard one wing at a time. I'd have to return when the side of the Museum I wanted to see was open. Deeply disappointed, I took the commuter train back up to Chestnut Hill and hitched a ride -- you could do that back then -- to where I was staying with my parents.

On a day I knew the wing of the Museum I wanted to see *should* be open, I headed back into Center City. After I entered the Museum, I aimed for the right wing, which was to my left, and which was, as I had hoped, open. I walked through the Arensberg Collection where Duchamp's paintings and constructs were displayed, checking them out in a cursory fashion as my eyes were focused on the prize. The building was still empty; I passed only one or two guards, and finally reached a dead end. In this room there was a large wooden farm door, though in truth it was more like a castle gate. It was made of thick planks surrounded by a stone archway. When I walked up to it, I noticed two tiny holes had been drilled in the middle. I looked through them. And saw the most wonderful sight. It was a naked female mannequin, her face obscured by the broken bricks framing the scene, reclining in a field of fake grass, holding aloft a tiny gaslight, which was lit. Behind this tableau was a painted landscape depicting a waterfall. It was obviously an appropriation of the Statue of Liberty – Duchamp's cry for real freedom in the land of the not-so-free. It was not only a tremendous work of art; what he had done was truly funny! I cracked up, laughing out loud.

A guard rounded the corner with a stern look on his face and wondered what was up.

"I've just seen God," I told him and left the room.

Size Matters

I moved to Manhattan after I finished college and my service as a VISTA Volunteer. I lucked out and found an apartment in Hell's Kitchen, very close to Times Square. Hell's Kitchen was the only neighborhood in New York City I knew anything about because it was near the Port Authority Bus Terminal. Back when I was enrolled in Albright College in Reading, Pennsylvania, I studied drama and the professor who taught the class would charter buses to the Port Authority and then walk us over to Times Square to see plays. He always chose the most outrageous ones because he was trying to teach us to rebel against the status quo. His favorite playwright was Bertolt Brecht. After class, we'd gossip in the hall, and we all pretty much agreed that our professor, on some level, considered himself to be Brecht reincarnated.

One of the plays he took us to was *Hair*. That evening kind of shocked me because the actors and actresses were telling us to be free and live a hippy lifestyle, but the audience was basically men and women in tuxedoes and evening gowns. There was such a disconnect! Our professor ran up and down the aisles waving his arms and cheering, but we looked at him and at each other and just shrugged. At the end of the night, we took a bus back to Pennsylvania.

After settling into my new living space, I started looking for a job. I also wanted to sample the incredible culture that was now surrounding me. In college, I took a lot of literature classes and had been introduced to the works of James Joyce, among others. He was now my favorite author and I heard that there was a James Joyce Society that met at the Gotham Book Mart bookstore. I went there several times to buy copies of his books.

As the weeks went by, I didn't have any luck finding employment. I was getting desperate, so I decided to head over to the Gotham Book Mart to see if they were hiring. After several minutes of browsing through the *Selected Letters of James Joyce*, I approached one of the managers and inquired about the possibility of working there. "Sure," he replied. He turned and pointed to a very small table with a typewriter on it surrounded by many tall stacks of books. There was a tiny steel chair almost hidden beneath it. "If you can fit, you got the job." I couldn't and didn't, so I left, very disappointed.

Luckily the Strand Bookstore, a much larger store, eventually hired me, so I was able to remain a New Yorker.

Building a Library

The bookstore I was working in when I built the bulk of my current library was the Strand; a huge un-air-conditioned warehouse full of dusty old used books. Over the course of a year almost every book ever written turned up there. Widows sold them the libraries of their dead husbands, reviewers brought them their unread review copies, and junkies schlepped in with torn shopping bags full of stolen books ripped off from Lower East Side tenements. The owner and his son bought them all. And they all had to be priced and shelved. I was one of the shelvers. This meant that I was one of the first employees allowed to go through the individual tomes looking for artifacts and minutiae -- letters, interesting bookmarks, ticket stubs, photographs, etc. I crammed all these found objects into my pockets and used them in my writing projects when I got home, treating the material both as building blocks and kismetic guides -- I still have scrapbooks filled with this stuff.

I also collected books on human offal: *The Smallest Room* by Pudney, *Clean and Decent* by Lawrence Wright, *Cleanliness and Godliness - or The Further Metamorphosis - A Discussion of the Problems of Sanitation raised by Sir John Harington, together with Reflections upon Further Progress recorded since that Excellent Knight, by his Invention of the Metamorphosed Ajax, Father of Conveniences, revolutionised the System of Sanitation in this country etc.* by Reginald Reynolds (Ajax comes from the word 'jakes,' British slang for outhouse). I also bought the Bantam paperback containing the MIT study for building better toilets -- it had diagrams of the splash patterns one created when pissing into old-fashioned urinals, and explained what could be done, design-wise, to keep those droplets off your shoes in the future. I also picked up a tiny cloth-bound gift book on Thomas Crapper, the Englishman who gave his name to our daily dumps. I should point out that these books were, and still are, worth a lot of money. Anyway, once you start talking about turds at play, particularly *Homeric* turds in motion, you end up, inevitably, mentioning Ben Jonson's 'On the Famous Voyage,' a long poem in which two wits row up the Fleet Street Ditch, an open sewer, commenting on all the shitting going on as they pass by.

I wrote copious notes for my various literary projects throughout the day, scribbling sentences on torn scraps of paper and inking messages on the palms of my hands. By this time, mid-'72, I was living in New Jersey -- exit ten on the turnpike. The commute back and forth to my lousy little bookstore job was daunting. It took an hour and a half each way -- that's three hours of death subtracted daily from what was something less than the ideal life. Going to work wasn't so bad, though it was way too early in the morning. Getting home was another story. To catch the 7:05 Suburban Transit bus to Edison I'd have to dash out of the store at closing time, 6:30 on the dot, jog up to the Union Square subway station, grab an 'R' or an 'N' train, walk through the cars from the last to the first to save some time, pushing through the rush hour crush, get out at 42nd Street, then run through the twisting maze of underground passageways that led to the Port Authority Bus Terminal on 8th Avenue. By the time I clambered onto the bus I was a sweaty nervous wreck. I'd sit there drenched, in my dirty t-shirt and jeans, among the well-dressed business commuters like a cancer cell among the healthy. Hell, because I was always the last person to get on, I'd almost always end up on the engine-hump seat in the rear -- the hottest, most cramped spot on the bus. I would sit there writing furiously, in a vain attempt to make my life meaningful, transcribing the notes I'd made earlier at work, trying to turn them into something usable.

The third part of this literary trifecta -- first part; collecting material at work, second; organizing it on the bus ride home -- began when I got back to the sleazy sub-division I lived in: this was the typing part, trying to come up with a couple of pages, even a couple of paragraphs, of serviceable prose. The bus stop where I got off was at a strip-mall parking lot near the two-storied box that contained the apartment. The mall had a 7-Eleven, where I'd pick up milk and soda and Nabisco Peanut Butter Creme Patties, my favorite snack. I was gaining a lot of weight eating this junk, but things were so fucked up in other ways that this was only a minor irritant.

After dinner, I'd sit down at the ancient blue portable typewriter that had gotten me through college. It was mostly plastic, with no heft, but I could bang the shit out of it. I used corrasable paper and, as I was constantly rewriting as I went along, my tiny, much-abused typer was filling with eraser shavings.

This is a piece I wrote using notes, and letters, and postcards from used books I shelved in the literature section of the Strand. It was originally published in *the Brooklyn Rail* accompanied by photographs of the original items.

My Father

My father sailed the seas.

He spent the bulk of his years on ornately appointed ocean liners, rusting freighters and scarred men-of-war, bobbing over the waves. He was born Victor Radio in West Orange, New Jersey, on a rainy inauspicious afternoon in April 1898, to Hadley Radio and Myrna Radio, nee Sebniewski, formerly of New York City.

I have a picture of him at the age of twelve, before the sun permanently creased his face, in knee socks, knickers and ankle-length boots, standing on a well-tended lawn, holding a golf club longer than he was tall; his steel-rimmed glasses framing a smile for the camera. He joined the Merchant Marine as a wireless operator in 1914. He must have been big for his years even then.

He got torpedoed twice during the Great War, once right off the coast of New Jersey, not far from the boardwalks of Atlantic City, in front of an audience of startled bathers.

He met my mother-to-be, Olivia Swickley, at a 1922 performance of the *Lumia Suite*, with Thomas Wilford himself at the Clavilux, the gentle flowing figures of light bringing them together. He had just returned from a run to Glasgow, delivering a cargo of wool, I think. He gave her a picture of the Necropolis, mounted on cardboard; graphically depicting the famous levels of the dead, tier upon tier of them, gothic mausoleums towering over the flat headstones in the foreground.

"Keep your face toward the Sunshine and the Shadows will fall behind You." He wrote these romantic lines to her in the fall of 1937. On July 29, 1938, he purchased a ticket from the New York Central Railroad to White Plains, New Jersey, at which time he proposed to her a joining of their fortunes and futures.

I think the match broke her father's, my grandfather's, heart, for he drove his model 'T' down the railroad tracks late one night into a highballing express. All they ever found of him was a small lingering cloud of alcohol.

The last time my fragile Mother laid eyes on my sea-faring Father was at the three o'clock show on Monday, January 29, 1940, at the Grand Ballroom of the Waldorf-Astoria Hotel in New York City, where he accompanied her to a talk given by Mr. David Burpee and saw the preview of his New Tetra Marigold. My mother, I should explain, loved flowers, and often produced intricate arrangements of fascinating designs. I still have their admission card yet. Admit two, it states in boldface type on the bottom border.

Promptly after the show my father, already wizened from constant squinting over brilliant watery expanses, shipped out on the good ship *Klactoveededstene*. Never known for his jocoseness, he merely chucked my mother under the chin, kissed her briefly, and was gone.

She never saw him again.

I can visualize him sitting in a spindly wooden deckchair, a blanket of plaid tucked under his legs, a scarf wrapped around his thick neck, a wide-brimmed sports cap upon his graying hair, reading a book slowly. Peering through his steel-rimmed glasses misted with sea spray.

"You have no idea what it was like to love a King-sized man," my mother often told me. "It meant king-sized beds, aisle seats at the movies, running when he walked, holding your breath when he tried on new clothes; for they never seemed to fit."

There are probably miles from Peru in steerage, and coils of hemp, barrels of syrup and ingots of copper in the bay. The hold exudes the smell of mule dung.

His large head shifts from side to side with the lazy swells of the sea. A breeze tugs at the corners of his blanket and flutters the bill of his hat. A pipe dangles loosely in his paw. He knocks the ashes from it against the leg of his chair and watches them skip across the deck.

The crew is foreign-born.

The days have been too bright, and too warm, for him.

Someday the sea will rise, a churning mass, and the pages of his book will flip past in a blur, too fast for his aging eyes to follow, his blanket in tatters, strips of cloth dancing wildly in the wind, his scarf blown away.

Northwesters.

Squalls.

They've drawn a circle in chalk around his chair.

And he remembers those days when but the simple act of throwing his book overboard would have put diamonds in the sea.

The Bust

I got fired from my job at the Strand Bookstore -- but it was for a crime I didn't commit. I was working the cash register in the front of the store and noticed an expensive leather-bound set of Dickens' letters, wrapped in brown paper, on the counter in front of me. I figured it had been sent down from the rare books room on the fifth floor and was waiting for a customer to come in and pick it up. It was an extremely slow day, so I started doodling with a ballpoint pen on the wrapping.

From out of nowhere, two hands appeared, grabbed at the parcel and tried to snatch it from the counter. I held it in place and looked up to see what was going on. I was surprised to find myself staring at the face of an ex-employee. This particular ex-employee was a strange dude from the mid-west who wore size 17 Converse and resembled Civil War soldiers I'd seen in old photographs. I sometimes thought that if reincarnation was real, that's what he had been.

And he *was* a thief – a very clever thief. He was in charge of taking books that had been ordered by mail to the post office on Fourth Avenue and paying to have them shipped to out-of-state customers. On one of his trips, he'd reached into a postal clerk's window when his back was turned and scooped up a receipt book. He would pay, let's say, fifty dollars for a mailing, write seventy-five on his own copy of the receipt, tossing away the real one, and pocket the difference. He'd then wheel his mail cart over to the Albert Hotel on University Place where he lived, park it outside, take a bunch of books he hadn't paid for up to his room, and then return to the store. He was efficient, so only a few of us knew what he was up to and, as we weren't snitches, nobody told on him. More to the point; he was very strong and very crazy, and those are the real reasons nobody spilled the beans. He was finally let go because one of the managers sort of suspected something, or just because he was so weird.

Anyway, he glared at me and told me he was taking the Dickens.

"Man, you can't do that! That's stealing! I'll get fired!"

"Oh, all right! Here you go," he said, tossing a crumpled-up ten-dollar bill over the counter, where it fell to the floor. When I bent over to pick it up, he grabbed the package and left.

It turned out that the manager who had gotten him fired had been tailing him, witnessed the entire transaction, and thought I was in cahoots with the thief. So I got fired; no matter how much I protested and tried to explain what had really happened.

I filed for unemployment but was told that my former employer was blocking any payments. I panicked; I was living pretty close to the edge, and the store wasn't paying me all that much as it was – I sure hadn't managed to save anything. I figured I might be able set things straight by getting the books back to the store. I took a couple of friends along in case things got physical and went over to the Albert Hotel. My friends kept out of sight in the stairwell while I banged on his door.

Much to my surprise, he opened the door and let me in. His room was unfurnished -- there was just this massive pile of books and boxes in the center of the floor, which was bare. There seemed to be some kind of sleeping bag next to it with a blanket strewn on top. I looked around, still kind of surprised to be there, and noticed that there was a mantel on the wall to the right of the door over a fake fireplace, with stuff on it – some candles and what looked like a bust. I walked over for a closer look and discovered that it was a black marble bust of Adolf Hitler. I mumbled something or other about my financial situation, and how desperate I was, but I couldn't focus; I was shaking. He seemed to sense my extreme unease, and must have felt sorry for me, because he gave me back the Dickens, still wrapped in the brown paper covered with my doodles.

I clutched the package and staggered out into the hallway feeling like I'd been punched in the chest by a massive dark fist.

Man in the Grey Flannel Beret

In the late 70s I was a stoned-out ex-hippy working in New Morning bookstore in pre-gentrified Soho. I had long hair, a peace sign dangling from a leather lanyard around my neck and a dog-eared copy of *Howl* in my back pocket. Luckily for me, the bookstore was owned by High Times magazine, so the job was very low-key. They'd even let us close the cash register and have poetry readings.

One warm summer evening Allen Ginsberg read there. After the reading, Ginsberg invited us to accompany him to the Spring Street Bar for some beers.

Man, I got so excited! I was finally going to hear firsthand those rumored stories about wild sex in freight cars, drug-crazed nights in exotic Mexican jungles and gay hustling on the Four-O-Deuce. I locked up the store and joined the rest of the staff as we eagerly followed the poet across the street to the bar. But the conversation didn't go at all the way I thought it would.

Ginsberg proceeded to minutely detail for our enjoyment his book and record deals -- how many tenths of a cent he got per copy of *Howl* sold. I got thoroughly drunk and left; disappointed, but still loving my beat-up copy of *Howl* -- Allen had signed it, and then drawn a cartoon of a flower under his signature before we'd left the store.

###

By the mid-80s I was working at St. Mark's Bookshop on St. Mark's Place. I had a buzz cut and wore a black leather jacket. Ginsberg's *Collected Poems* had just been published in an expensive hardcover edition, and we were doing a brisk business with the red dust-jacketed item.

The store's owner gave me Ginsberg's phone number and told me to call him and ask him to stop by and sign copies of his book. Books signed by their authors usually sell faster than unsigned ones – they're simply more valuable. I said ok, and when I had a spare moment I dialed the number. Ginsberg answered -- that was my first surprise – I'd expected an answering machine or some kind of intermediary.

"Hi, Mr. Ginsberg," I said. "Is there any chance you could come by the bookstore and sign copies of your new book?"

"Sure," he said, "but only if you can tell me exactly how many copies have sold."

"I don't know," I answered truthfully, somewhat taken aback.

"Well, you'd better find out," he said, "if you want to see me any time in the near future."

"Just a minute – I'll ask the boss," I said in a panic, knowing I'd be in trouble if I messed this up. The owner would not be happy -- I'd be dusting bookshelves the rest of my shift. I put my hand over the receiver and asked the other clerks if anyone knew exactly has many copies of Ginsberg's *Collected Works* we'd already sold. Nobody had a clue. I took my hand off the receiver and said, "Fifty."

"Great," he said. "I'll be right over."

Privates

I used to go to clubs and hear a lot of music. One of the clubs I went to was called Privates on 85th Street on the Upper East Side. Once it had been a private school, but that had closed, and now it was a cool place to see bands. A lot of great music happened there – from Bo Diddley to the Specials.

Because of my bookstore connections, I got invited to an exclusive William Burroughs event that was scheduled to take place in that venue. At the time I was managing New Morning, a bookstore in Soho named after the Bob Dylan album. It was owned by *High Times* magazine, and for that reason, it was considered 'hip.' We made sure we always had a complete run of William Burroughs' books in stock – his work, published by Grove Press, was very popular.

So I was thrilled at getting the chance to see him, a writer I admired, in person. I had always considered Burroughs to be the American Celine, another writer I loved, and I figured that Allen Ginsberg must have felt the same way. Ginsberg seemed to surround himself with archetypes: He took along only one in each category on his extended Beatnik trip. Anne Waldman was the token woman, Corso was the crazy dude, and Burroughs was the European experimental prose writer – the European *intellectual* experimental prose writer.

I got there just as Burroughs was making his grand entrance, and to this day that scene lives vividly in my mind. He came in with an entourage; an army of very young men, all of them about the same height, and all very well dressed. They crowded around Bill, which seemed to raise him up, so that his feet barely touched the floor. There was a humming sound emanating from them as they passed by -- it was like the buzzing of a cluster of worker bees carrying the Queen to her throne in the hive. They escorted him to what looked like a gazebo, a small round structure in the middle of the hall, and then the celebration ensued. I got loaded and the rest of that evening was just a blur.

Philip Roth

I met Philip Roth when I was working at Coliseum Books, on the corner of 57th Street and Broadway. Coliseum was one of the largest bookstores in Manhattan at the time and was the place to go if you were a serious lover of books.

Coliseum was also at the top of the list of places to make an appearance for published authors, particularly best-selling ones. The tiny, grizzled Norman Mailer came by the store, escorted by his statuesque wife, Norris Church, who walked him like a wayward bulldog up the steep steps to the manager's station, where we had piled copies of his books to be signed. He grumbled but signed them anyway.

Then there was the time the famous novelist, Philip Roth, stopped by. The store manager, who was star-struck, let him walk up the three steps that led behind the counters where the cashiers and the cash registers were.

There was a long plate-glass window overlooking Broadway behind them, and the early afternoon sun would shine brightly through it. This same sun was now etching a fiery halo around Philip Roth's head and shoulders as I looked up at him. I was stuck dumb by the vision before me. I so wanted to ask him about one of his early books, *Letting Go*, that had played an important part in my life when I was in college, but I simply couldn't get the words to come out. He thanked the store manager, turned and left.

He visited the store many times after that, as he lived on the Upper West Side. I'd say 'hello' to him, and that was about it. I never did get a chance to engage him in a conversation about *Letting Go* before he passed away.

A friend of mine, Arthur Kaye, who worked in the Strand Bookstore after I left, got introduced to Erica Heller, Joseph Heller's daughter, through the store. She invited him to submit a piece to a literary project she was working on: lunches with famous dead people as if they were still alive. Arthur told her about me, and she said that I could submit a piece, too. After Arthur filled me in, and after thinking about it for a couple of days, I composed a story featuring me and Philip Roth, who I knew only superficially, enjoying a late lunch at The Russian Tea Room which, in real life, wasn't that far away from Coliseum Bookstore where I was now employed, and where I had briefly met him.

Erica was very supportive, and we swapped many emails about my piece – I even dropped off some of my books to her doorman at the Ansonia on the Upper Westside. But things didn't work out in the end. Both Arthur and I got rejected in the final cut – because we weren't famous enough ourselves. Her book, *One Last Lunch*, was finally published, and I recommend it, as it is very interesting and revealing! My story, 'My Lunch with the Late Philip Roth', did finally see the light of day, in Sanjay Agnihotri's wonderful journal, *Local Knowledge*.

And here it is:

My Lunch with the Late Philip Roth

Philip Roth is sitting at the table with me in The Russian Tea Room and he's wielding his knife and fork with dispatch on the mound of food on his plate. He ordered *Cotelette a la Kiev* with Yukon mashed potatoes – one of their famous entrees – priced at a mere forty-two dollars. I went with an appetizer; the traditional Tea Room Red Borscht – priced at only twenty-four dollars. I have to remind myself as I eat that I am sitting across from a person who is no more -- who is deceased.

I'd met the late, great novelist, Philip Roth, at the bar in the front of the restaurant around two in the afternoon. I figured that after a couple of drinks, we would proceed to a booth and order lunch. I'd called the maître d' earlier in the day, and asked her if there was a dress code, and she said no, forget about what you might have read online. I probably should have also asked if it was ok to have alcohol and food with a dead man, but I let that one go. So I'd dressed in a cotton shirt and black jeans, unlike Mr. Roth, who was formidable in his dark suit, though that does make some sort of sense, given where he'd come from. To the best of my recollection, he'd always been well-attired whenever I'd run into him in the past. Just in case he'd forgotten who I was, and why we both were there, I introduced myself.

"Hi, Mr. Roth," I said to him. "I recognized you right away! You look great, all things considered. Just to remind you, my name is Ron Kolm. We met several times years ago in the old Coliseum Bookstore. You were always very personable to me, a mere bookstore clerk. More recently, we've exchanged a number of emails. What do you want to drink?"

"Call me Philip," he said, "and I'll have a *Bactika 3*, it's Russian, and only costs eighteen bucks a bottle – and, as we agreed in our emails, you'll be treating me. You have no idea how difficult this process of escaping the nether zone is, even for a brief while!"

"No problem. I still have a little room left on one of my credit cards, and having this chance to actually talk to you at length, and ask you some questions about one of your earlier books, *Letting Go*, totally makes paying for everything worthwhile!"

"Right, but I don't want to talk about that one. I'm much more curious about which of my books are selling now, and what you hear from customers about my suddenly rather controversial book, *The Plot Against America*. *That's* the one that should have gotten me the Nobel Prize! I mean really – what's *with* those people? Anyway, everyone in the dead zone, or whatever you want to call it, has a copy, and damn, everyone's copy is kind of beat up – nobody takes care of their possessions in the afterlife."

"Well, for what it's worth, I just bought a brand-new paperback copy from..."

"Yeah, yeah. Posman Books. I know where you work. Down there, where I currently reside, we know everything – knowledge is like a virus there – someone learns something and we all know it right away. It's because of your bookstore job that I invited you to meet me here."

"Sorry to interrupt you, but do you still want that beer? The bartender seems to be waving in our direction. Or do you want to order lunch now? The Prix-Fixe is fifty-five dollars, and it's served until four-thirty."

"I'll have a beer," he replied, so I ordered two. He then nervously added, "Do you see any screens around us? On the wall behind the bottles? Thank God you don't have a laptop! I hate screens, period."

"Yeah, I read the article where you mentioned that. Shocked the hell out of me! You've published over thirty-one books, yet you seem to think that you'll be regarded as a cult figure years from now because of movies, TV, and computers. I did try to do some homework on my way here... um, I used my cellphone, so sorry."

"It's ok when you're reading stuff about *me* – in fact, that's a *good* thing. Hey, when you were doing your research, did you read about this place we're in? That the second booth off to the left of us is called the 'Tootsie Booth' because of the movie? It was actually filmed here."

"Is that why you picked this place to meet?" I asked.

"No. It's because of the Russian collusion thing. I hate Donald Trump and everything he stands for. That guy has a vocabulary of seventy-seven words, and even that's stretching it. He doesn't know *anything* about government, history, science or philosophy. I call the way he speaks, 'Jerkish.' Getting back to my book, and the anxious and fear-ridden families depicted in it, what is most terrifying is that Trump makes any and everything possible, including, of course, the nuclear catastrophe."

"Man, I remember reading almost those exact words in an article that was quoting you."

"Yeah, I know, but those are my words, and I can use them as many times as I want to. There are no rules regarding what we do in the shadow world. Trump will fit in nicely when he gets there!"

"The sooner the better, in my opinion. Now, back to what you want to eat for lunch..."

"Chicken Kiev," he said, as we left the bar, beers in hand, and made our way back to the 'Tootsie Booth.'

Our conversation continues intermittently while we're eating. The food is well-prepared, and very tasty. I probably should have ordered an entrée, too, as my plate is now empty, except for a boiled potato, looking very lonely.

"A quick question," I say, glancing at a dessert menu. "Since you can see everything from where you are now, what's the story on the 'Pee Tape?' And as far at that collusion thing goes – which you mentioned…"

"I'm not allowed to talk about any of that, really. I can joke about those things – that's ok. I love telling jokes, by the way. I got into doing that after a bad period in my life. Doing a sort of stand-up with my friends led directly to *Portnoy*," he says smirking, as he shoves another forkful of breaded chicken into his mouth.

"Well, I haven't been able to eat liver since I read that book. I still like the smell of it cooking, but you know…"

After roughly an hour of conversation, he begins to drift out of focus, much like a cloudy image on an old television screen. I look down at the boiled potato still sitting on my plate and try to figure out what the final tally on the bill will be. I never did order dessert; I couldn't afford to.

"I probably have gone too far and said too much." He smiles again, faintly, before taking a final bite of chicken. His plate is almost spotless. "Please do your best to keep my books in stock," he says, getting up from the table and bowing slightly. He shakes my hand, whirls around and walks briskly away, disappearing into a mist as he does so. I stare after him. My stomach does somersaults as the waitress hands me the check.

46

Ugly George

When cable TV was brand new, there was a guy with a local show in New York who called himself 'Ugly George.' And it's true; he wasn't very attractive. He had a sweaty tangle of black stringy hair, a squirrelly look, and his portable camera was a battered piece of crap; all wrapped in tape.

Anyway, Ugly George would cruise the city looking for attractive women. His territory was the back streets, where there wasn't a lot of foot traffic to contend with. When he found one, he'd approach her and ask if she would remove her top and show him, and by extension his audience, her tits. Most said 'no.' but every now and again he got lucky. I thought he was a slimy sexist pig, and I detested him.

One day he wandered into Coliseum Books, the store I was working in at the time, and he approached one of the cashiers in the front of the store. I lost it. I rolled up my T-shirt and walked briskly up to him.

"Hey, you big piece of shit, what do you think of these?" I snarled, shaking my bare chest.

"Don't do this to me!" he cried, turning and fleeing the store.

I chased him up Broadway, rubbing my nipples. I can't tell you how good the cool air felt on them.

THE INTERVIEW

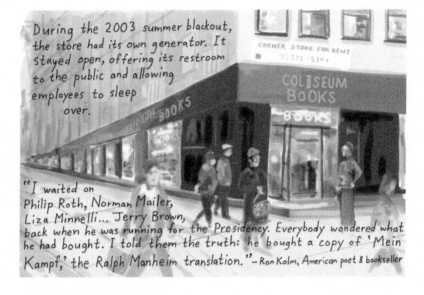

During the 2003 summer blackout, the store had its own generator. It stayed open, offering its restroom to the public and allowing employees to sleep over.

"I waited on Philip Roth, Norman Mailer, Liza Minnelli... Jerry Brown, back when he was running for the Presidency. Everybody wondered what he had bought. I told them the truth: he bought a copy of 'Mein Kampf,' the Ralph Manheim translation." —Ron Kolm, American poet & bookseller

Coliseum Books Interview with
Ron Kolm

by Kathryn Adisman

From the diary of "Parker" K Madisan recovered
from the rubble of the Coliseum: *January 2002. I'm
standing on the corner of 57th Street and Broadway
under the awning of Pax Deli, rain coming down,
waiting for night manager of the bookstore Ron
Kolm, "with an M" he says on the phone, "as in
Manhattan." Across the street the slanting yellow
banner of the Coliseum Books sign glares at me. Talk
about bad omens. When the Coliseum falls... A big
chunk of the Manhattan landscape is about to vanish
forever, and I'm here to get the story.*

Ron Kolm is one of the founding members of The
Unbearables, a group of writers who formed in the
mid-'80s as an act of rebellion against the literary
establishment – "mildly famous" for picketing The
New Yorker and for the annual reading of erotic
poems on the Brooklyn Bridge. Kolm, who is tall yet
self-effacing, with his trademark mustache and
glasses, a combination of approachable and
knowledgeable (ideal in a bookseller), always thinks
of himself as a writer first and foremost.

Yet he's spent a lifetime working in NYC's
independent bookstores – The Strand in the '70s (he
recalls the weekly starting salary was $60), East Side
Books, Saint Mark's Bookshop and New Morning
owned by High Times) that later became Spring
Street Books ("I would have worked at Gotham Book

Mart, except my feet didn't fit in the space behind the front counter."). Between 1981 and 2002, he was a night manager at Coliseum Bookstore for a total of 18 years where he witnessed the changes in NYC firsthand.

The Big Picture, according to Kolm, who admits he has a habit of philosophizing, is: "America has become the very thing it had initially rebelled against – an Imperial Empire." Kolm sees the store closing as a portent of the end of alternative institutions. For example, the neighborhood Irish bar, Shandon Star, turned into a Wendy's.

"It's the end of an era," Kolm predicts. "Coliseum Books is a blue-collar bookstore." He points to his work attire: "I wear a blue-collar shirt and blue jeans!" He calls the store "a populist institution. It has the books people want, and if we don't have them, we can order them. The staff knows books – they actually read them. It's just a really great bookstore."

As the culture became more and more upscale, "Coliseum is one of the final victims of the gentrification of New York – a town commons vs. Barnes & Nobles, an entertainment complex. Though I guess the chains do have their place." Ron says sheepishly, as he confesses to doing a poetry reading at a Barnes & Noble! Back in the day, when Coliseum Books arrived, pre-Barnes & Noble, it was the superstore on the block, and this was a car dealership neighborhood, heavy on crime. The night staff were like bouncers. Ron regales me with tales of heroic acts in the service of preserving books from thieves. "One guy in a Panama hat had a machete in his bag." There are few women employees except cashiers ("estrogen behind a moat," he says, jokingly) – a throwback to when Times Square was "really rough." He admits sexism is a problem but stresses the staff's ethnic diversity.

Media blitz:

"It began with a piece in The Daily News, picked up by AP, Channel 9, 11, 1010 WINS radio...*The Village Voice* ... the *LA Times*. By December 29, the place was mobbed." At first, he just saw it as something closing, but now looks at it differently. "It was the only possible outcome," says Kolm, "given the personality of the leading players" – an uncompromising bookstore owner vs. a wealthy Iranian landlord banking on economic turnaround with the AOL Time Warner tower going up on the former site of the Coliseum at Columbus Circle. "This was almost the stuff of Greek tragedy. I'm amazed at the depth of feeling among customers, who are sad and angry: they offer to sign a petition, make a phone call. People educate themselves on the premises." While the store may disappear from the neighborhood, "The book," says Kolm, "is an artifact. It will live forever."

"A bit of a bibliophile," Ron sold 30 cartons of books to NYU for $10,000. The Fales Collection at the New York University Library sent a truck over to pick up his collection. He got written up in *The New York Times*. "What I collected were runs of magazines. *Between C&D* and *Red Tape*. I had all of Lynn Tillman's books and Kathy Acker's. I had signed Art Spiegelman stuff. Because I knew those people. But it finally hit me that all of this material was just sitting in boxes in my apartment, where nobody could access it, so I made the decision to try to find a place where it could be archived, thus NYU."

"I have always looked at writing as communicating. I've got stories and substories. But many of my stories do take place in New York City, and the city is depicted as being different from the rest of the United States. It's a place you can come to and reinvent yourself. That's what I did. I came from Pennsylvania where everyone told you, you were a certain way. But I had heard that you could come to New York and be anything you wanted to be. You could start fresh. And now the city is reinventing itself, too. It's going to be interesting to see what it becomes again after this. It's not like the rest of the United States …"

He takes a cyclical perspective, "I've seen the city go from one thing to something completely far removed from that thing." After 9/11, he foresees a return to white flight, with yuppies leaving. But the real New Yorkers – folks like Fran Lebowitz and Tuli Kupferberg of the Fugs – what he calls "the substrata" – will remain.

###

So there you have it straight from the horse's mouth! Decades in the future, if anyone is reading this in the archives at Fales Library, where it's been preserved, and wonders: Whatever happened to America, in the wake of 9/11? Whatever happened to NYC? Just remember what Ron Kolm said at the Fall of Coliseum Books.

POEMS

Hell's Kitchen

> For Fred Bass, the owner of the
> Strand Bookstore, who gave me a job
> when I desperately needed one

After the war in Vietnam
wound down, and my stint
doing alternative service
came to an end,
I had to stop
and take stock
of my situation.
I could return to Pennsylvania
and get a job in a factory
dealing with chemicals
that fuck with your body,
but I'd done that before
I signed up for Appalachia
and it sure wasn't much fun
back then, so I decided
not to go that route again.

Also, I was starting
to think of myself as a writer,
and to pursue that career
I figured I have to move
to New York City
because I'd heard
that's where the action was.

My pick-up truck
had thousands of miles on it
and wasn't going to last

much longer, but
I knew I could use it
for one more mission.

I loaded it up
with the many boxes
of books I'd bought
during my travels
across the country
and a bag of clothes
and headed north.

I drove to the Port Authority,
parked, and went outside
to look for a newspaper.
I found a copy
of *the Village Voice*
and took it back to the truck
where I checked out
the apartment listings.

I found several, but the one
that interested me the most
was for a studio on 46th Street,
between 8th and 9th Avenues,
for a hundred and sixty a month.
I circled the phone number
and called it from a pay phone.

I managed to get
an immediate appointment
to check the joint out.
I liked what I saw, plus

I could afford it, having
saved some money
from my year of service.
I signed a two-year lease,
and gave the landlord a check.

I went back to the parking lot
got my vehicle
drove to the street
in front of my new place
and carried my stuff inside.

I woke up the next morning
after a fitful night's sleep
on the bare floor, and
started looking for a job,
but nothing went my way.
Every place I applied to
seemed interested at first
but as soon as I got to the part
where I told them about
my year in VISTA
they got cold feet.
I could read the equation
on their faces—
community organizer
equals union organizer—
and nobody wanted that.

The days went by
and my savings
were dwindling,
so I started selling off

parts of my library
to get enough cash
for food and rent.

I became one of the regulars
at the Strand Bookstore
and Fred, the owner's son,
began to recognize me.
After my third trip,
he offered me a job,
but as the pay
was sixty dollars a week,
I said no, and continued
to pound the pavement
to no effect.

After my fifth trip
I said yes.
I was running out of books.

CBGBs

I worked in the Strand bookstore
with Tom Verlaine. He invited me
to CBGBs the first time his band,
Television, played there.
Punk was born that night.
I ended up getting into a fight
with my date, and we left
to take it outside.
Tom yelled at me the next day,
"Why the *fuck* did you split?"
I responded by asking
how the hell he knew I'd left.
"I can see *everything* from the stage,"
he answered,
as he continued to shelve books.

Me and Patti Smith

For a brief while
Patti Smith and I shelved books
in the Strand Bookstore
at the same time.
I did get the chance to see her perform
with Lenny Kaye playing guitar
on a rooftop high above Grand Street,
but our main interaction happened
when she strode up to me in the store
and thrust the Caedmon recording
of James Joyce reading
into my hands.
"Someone told me I looked like him
and gave me this – That's bullshit!
I heard you like him, so it's yours!"
I still have that record
in my collection.

Yet Another Strange Customer

I'm arranging used books
just purchased by the owner
in the Strand Bookstore
when a priest joins me
at the front sales table.
"I love to tend the dying,"
he says, tugging
at my sleeve,
"And in the end
I always manage
a fine impromptu anguish."
He touches my shoulder
and whispers,
"I can even
call your enemies by name."
I twist away from him,
hoping he'll disappear
so I can continue working.
"I studied the science of
beautiful thoughts when I
was just a novice," he cries,
vanishing back into the stacks,
"I could break your heart!"

**The Philosophy of Andy Warhol
(From A to B and Back Again)**

When I was working
in East Side Bookstore
on St. Mark's Place in the mid- '70s
one of my favorite books
was Andy Warhol's
*The Philosophy of Andy Warhol:
(From A to B and Back Again).*

When he got shot in the Factory
I was totally shocked.
I couldn't believe that anyone
would try to hurt him.
Anyway, one of my duties in the store
was to take books and 'zines
from neighborhood folks
and sell them on consignment.
They would eventually be paid
for what sold.

One afternoon a woman
came into the store, glared at me,
then slapped a small stack of books
on the counter
and said we had to sell them.

I picked up a copy.
It was the *SCUM Manifesto* by Valerie Solanas,
who was now staring at me intently.
I knew she was the person
who'd shot Andy Warhol

from watching the news on TV.
"Um, sure, we'll try to sell it,"
I told her nervously
and gave her a receipt.
She spun around and left the store.
I put her books on a rack,
mentally apologized to Andy Warhol,
and breathed a sigh of relief.

Classical Music Lover

It was a warm
late summer afternoon
in June, 1976,
and I was getting ready
to close the store
in about an hour.

The evening junkie group nod
had already started.
They'd shuffled in,
one after another,
and assumed their usual positions
in front of the poetry section
where they leaned
slowly forward
and then backward so far,
you'd think they'd fall
but they never did,
defying gravity for hours
until the end of the night.

When I had to close
I would gently tell them,
"You really do
have to leave now,"
but I never touched them
because I'd learned
from bitter experience
how badly it freaked them out—
they'd scream
and wave their arms around

knocking books off the shelves
and I'd have to beat a retreat
back to the cash register.

Anyway, I was listening
to The Velvet Underground,
my favorite band at the time
turned up real loud on the stereo
when a grizzled gentleman
stepped into my field of vision
glared at me, then snapped,
"Turn that shit off and play
some decent classical music!"
I almost said, "Fuck you!"
but I recognized him—
it was Charles Bukowski,
probably in town for a reading.
"I like this music and I'm not
taking it off," I said,
expecting an angry reply
but he surprised me
by apologizing instead.
"I'm sorry, I'm sorry, I'm sorry,"
he muttered, turning on his heels
and leaving the store.

To this day, I say everything
three times, a la Bukowski
and I wish I'd told him
how much I liked
his novel, *Post Office*,
which I've read
at least three times.

Incident in a NYC Bookstore

For Anne Waldman

I'm sitting behind the cash register
in East Side bookstore
on St. Mark's Place
near Second Avenue
looking at a postcard
that's taped to the wall
of Anne Waldman, topless.
It's been there a long time
but I've never actually read
the message she wrote on it.

So I'm kind of distracted
and I almost don't notice
a guy duck into the office
where the manager's bike
is chained to a desk.
I'm alone in the store
and I don't think Anne Waldman
will be coming to my rescue.

The guy comes out of the office
wheeling the bicycle –
he must have cut
the lock somehow.
"Hey," I shout at him,
as he approaches the door,
"That doesn't belong to you!
Put it back where you found it!"
He leans the bike
against a bookshelf

70

and slowly walks over
to where I'm perched
on my stool.

Gripping the edge of the counter
I look down at him. He's short
and stinks of alcohol--
his eyes glazed over.
But he lashes out
lightning fast
with a knife that sinks
into the top of my right hand.
The blade gets stuck in the cartilage
and he can't pull it out,
so he simply lets go
and stands there motionless,
like a toy whose battery has died.

There must be something
seriously wrong with me,
because I suddenly find myself
lecturing this neighborhood junkie.
"I could do anything I want to you,"
I tell him, picking up the club
we have under the counter
and waving it for emphasis.
"You're small and drunk and stupid.
I could probably even kill you
and get away with it,
but that would be pointless."
I yank the knife
out of my hand
and give it back to him.

"Just get the fuck out of here."
He exits the store,
slashing some flyers
posted near the door as he does so,
leaving me and Anne Waldman
alone again.

Metamorphosis

I'd been going through a terrible time
and everything I touched
seemed to break.
I was working in a bookstore
on 8th Street in Manhattan,
the only person on the night shift,
barely hanging on to the job.
Among the tasks I had to do
every evening after closing
was clean the bathroom.

Late one night I accidentally
knocked an empty vase
off the back of the toilet
and watched it crash
into the porcelain bowl
creating a constellation
of tiny slivers of glass.
"Fuck this shit! I'm out of here,"
I muttered, knowing
I'd probably be fired
for leaving such a mess
but at that moment I didn't care
as I was broken, too.

The next day
when I entered the store
the manager barked,
"Ron, we have to talk!"
I froze. He was taller than me,
and I'm pretty tall,

but he was staring down at me
waiting for my response.
Suddenly my mind started
racing like a cockroach
when you turn on the lights
as I tried to figure out
how to save my life.

In truth, the boss was actually
not a bad guy, but he kept
the good side of his personality
deeply buried so no one
could take advantage of him.
I desperately did my best
to reach that inner person.

"I know I did a bad thing last night,"
I said, looking up at him,
"And you can take the *easy* way out
and fire me or the much more *difficult*
and *rewarding* path of bearing with me
as I try to work through my problems."
He stood there quietly for a moment
glaring down at me, then relented.
"Sure," he replied. "We can do this.
Best of luck." After saying that,
he turned and walked away.
I clocked in and took my position
behind the cash register.

Another You

I thought we'd agreed
to meet in the bookstore
after I finished work.
I leaf through magazines,
killing time, waiting
for you to show up
and when you don't
I head downtown,
disappointed.

The club is jammed,
everyone dancing
to Fifties R&B.
I look over to the bar
and there you are
your back to the door
dressed in black
short blond hair.

I'm hungry for you,
but I'm angry, too.
"What's up," I say,
touching your back.
"Excuse me?" you say,
turning around and
I see it's really
not you at all.

Acker Awards

In 2013 I got an Acker Award
from Clayton Patterson for being
the Editor of the *Evergreen Review*
after Barney Rosset passed away.
I actually knew Kathy Acker back
in the day when I was managing
New Morning Bookstore in Soho.
She would stop by and ask to use
our only phone, talking on it for hours,
which made it difficult to place orders.
"I need to call a publisher." I'd beg.
"Sorry," she'd say. "I can't hang up –
I've got my agent on the line!"
And I'd go back to pricing books.

Winning Is Everything!

In 1992 Jerry Brown,
the liberal ex-governor of California,
ran against Bill Clinton
in the race to become
the Democratic party's nominee
for President of the United States.
He entered the New York primary
and came to New York City to campaign.
While he was here, he shopped
in Coliseum Bookstore on 57th Street
surrounded by a phalanx
of Secret Service agents.
When he approached the cash register
with a pile of books
I leaned over from my post
at the bag check counter
to see what he was buying.
At the top of the stack was a copy
of Adolf Hitler's *Mein Kampf*!
I was shocked. I wondered
if he actually thought Hitler's book
might contain some secrets
that would help him
win the election.

Armadillo Bookstore

For several weeks
I worked in a small bookstore
on the corner of West 10th
and Bleecker Street
in Greenwich Village.
One night a customer
approached the cash register
with a big stack of books
and asked if he could pay for them
with a personal check.
"Sure. But I have to see some ID.
It's the store policy," I told him.
"Isn't this enough?" he asked,
leaning forward and framing
his face with his hands.
I knew it was William Kunstler,
the famous radical lawyer,
but I wasn't impressed
by his macho display,
so I said, "No.
Please show me your identification."
Deflated, he took out his wallet.

The Beat Goes On

It was a slow night in the bookstore
so I went over to the literature section
and grabbed a copy of Celine's
Death on the Installment Plan
and took it back to my post
at the cash register.

I hid it under the counter
because we weren't supposed
to read on the job
and I didn't want to get fired.
But just as I opened the book
there was a loud banging on the front door.

I looked up and saw a disheveled man
throwing himself against it
rattling the glass panes.
"Aw crap," I muttered,
putting the book away
and leaving my seat
to deal with the problem.

I yanked the door open
and came face to face
with a broken human being
straight out of Celine.

When I reached out to restrain him,
a voice from behind me bellowed,
"Back off, Ron!
That's Gregory Corso,

the famous Beat poet!
I have a piece of his in the journal
I'm about to publish!"
"I'm so sorry," I said sheepishly.
"I had no idea."

The store's owner put his arm
around Corso's shoulder
and escorted him down the stairs
into the basement,
and I returned to Celine
who now seemed to be
right on the money.

Astor Place Station

I'd just dropped off
some consignment stuff
at St. Mark's Bookshop
and had fifteen minutes
to make it to Posman Books
in Grand Central Terminal
or I'd be late for work.

I got to the ornate
Astor Place entrance
to the uptown local and froze.
A sea of commuters
poured up the steps
and broke around me
like a wave on the beach.
I'd just missed a train.

I paid my fare and walked
up the empty platform.
As I approached the garbage bins
at the north end of the station
I passed a column and came
face to face with a dude
who was breathing heavily,
his back to the tracks.
I realized what was up right away
and, idiot that I am, pointed it out to him.
"Hey, you just jumped the rails
and crossed the tracks.
What's up with that?" I said,
smiling to show I was hip.

"I don't want to hurt you," he said,
staring right through me.
"Whoa, no problem! I said
nervously, "I'm cool!"
"I'm not going back to prison,"
he continued, unblinking.
"I'm down with that," I said,
my mind racing like a cockroach
when you turn on the lights.
"Do you like the Yankees?"
he asked, stunning me.
"Well, no, but I do like the Mets a bit,"
I answered stupidly, given the situation.
"I don't want to hurt you," he said again,
squaring his shoulders and striding off
towards the distant exit.

I looked down the platform
and saw figures with flashlights
searching the tracks.
I was getting later
and later for work, but
I didn't know what to do:
I'd made it through the Sixties
and I didn't want to betray
a brother to the man,
so I just stood there.

A number 6 train,
moving very slowly
finally pulled into the station
and I got on and sat down
shaking a little.

Across from me
leaning against a door
was the biggest transit cop
I'd ever seen, with a tiny
full-moon of a face,
all out of proportion.
I wanted to ask him
what had happened at the station
we were leaving behind
but I figured if it had been
something really bad
I'd be a material witness
so I kept my mouth shut
and went to work.

"I was looking out the front window and saw a crowd of people screaming and shouting as they ran up the ramp going to Forty-second and Vanderbilt—I figured that something bad must be happening in the station. Seconds later, just like in a Marx Brothers routine, they all came running back down, still shouting. We quickly asked the customers to leave and then locked the doors, evacuating through a rear entrance. When we reached the street, the sky was red and thick with dust—I thought a plane had hit a skyscraper, or that a building across from Grand

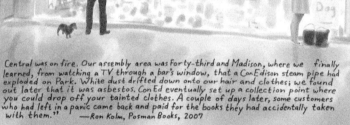

Central was on fire. Our assembly area was Forty-third and Madison, where we finally learned, from watching a TV through a bar's window, that a ConEdison steam pipe had exploded on Park. White dust drifted down onto our hair and clothes; we found out later that it was asbestos. ConEd eventually set up a collection point where you could drop off your tainted clothes. A couple of days later, some customers who had left in a panic came back and paid for the books they had accidentally taken with them." —Ron Kolm, Posman Books, 2007

Terminal

It's a quiet day
in Grand Central Station
and I'm killing time
at the information counter
looking stuff up
on the bookstore's computer.
There's a sudden commotion
outside the front window
as a crowd of people
runs up the ramp
towards 42nd Street
yelling and waving their arms.
Something must have gone
horribly wrong
in the terminal—
Maybe someone has a gun
or a bomb.
Perhaps it's the terrorist attack
we've been anticipating
for so long.
And just like that
they all come running
back down, still shouting,
just like in a Marx Brothers
movie, and this finally gets
the manager's attention.
Now even *he* knows
that something bad
has occurred.

As panic sets in
he gives the order
to evacuate the store.
We ask the customers
to please leave quickly.
A guy I work with
pulls me aside and says
he's going to slip out
the rear entrance --
Fuck everyone else!
I follow him
through the tunnels
over to the shuttle
where we exit the station.

When we reach street level
I see a horrendous sight:
The sky is blood red
and though it's summer
snowflakes are falling
and coating everything.
I figure that a plane
must have crashed
into a nearby building.
All I want to do
is flee this nightmare--
But we've been told
that if disaster strikes
we're supposed to assemble
on the corner of 43rd Street

and Madison where
a roll call will be taken
to make sure
everyone got out ok.
On my way there
I stop in a bar
to watch the news on TV
and finally find out
what really happened--
A Con Ed steam pipe had exploded
just a couple of blocks away
and shot debris high
into the surrounding sky.
I toss back a few
glued to the screen
and forget all about
the bookstore.

Days later
Con Edison announces
that the snow is asbestos,
and sets up a collection point
where contaminated clothes
can be dropped off
and put in garbage bags
to be buried somewhere--
But I can't afford
to trash mine
so I simply wash them
and hope for the best.

Garbage Run

One of my duties in the bookstore
is to take out the trash.
One night, not so long ago,
I was carrying a big stack
of flattened cardboard boxes
down the steep flight of steps
behind the store, when I slipped
and fell hard on my left hand.
A passer-by helped me up
and we both stared at my index finger,
which now resembled a swastika.

He walked me into the store
where the manager,
upon seeing my hand,
sent me immediately to the City MD
on 14th Street. The doctor there,
a young man, tried as hard as he could
to straighten my finger, but
nothing worked, so he sent me
to the near-by emergency room
at Mount Sinai Hospital.

It was a Saturday night in the West Village,
always an interesting time.
A bunch of disco refugees
staggered into the waiting room
looking for a toilet.
"Sorry, it's flooded," the guard said.
They didn't believe him, but they split,
calling him an asshole as they left.

A disheveled guy came in, probably
homeless, and sat down beside me.
He took off his right shoe, then his sock.
Then he popped his dislocated big toe
back into place. I envied him,
wishing I could do that
with my finger.

I was finally seen by a doctor
who looked at my hand,
sucked on her tongue, and said,
"I've seen this before."
She grabbed my index finger
and yanked it hard. There was
a tearing sound, but it worked.
I made a mental note that a woman
had succeeded where a man had failed,
thanked her immensely and went home.

It takes a pandemic

to end
a fifty-year career of working in
New York City's independent bookstores
which included The Strand, East Side Books,
New Morning, Coliseum Books, St. Mark's Bookshop
and Posman Books which closed on March 16th,
due to the virus. The last book I sold there
was Camus' *The Plague*.

(Thank you Steve Zeitlin and City Lore)

A Subway Story in the Time of COVID-19

I had to travel into Manhattan
to cash my unemployment check,
so I sat in the front car, wearing
a mask, doing my best
to avoid the other passengers.
After leaving the bank
I walked back to Union Square station
and found a place on the platform
where there weren't too many people
standing around waiting.

Time goes by and no train appears.
There's a sudden movement
as a woman, maybe late 50s,
tosses her bag and her mask onto the tracks,
then clumsily climbs down
and joins them.
"Hey, what's up?" I shout through my mask.
She moans and says
that this is how she's going to get home,
She's tired of everything.

She edges over towards the third rail,
and unfortunately
because my back
is so messed up
I can't physically grab her
so I unleash my best zinger,
"Do you believe in any kind of God?
Because if you do, you gotta know
how pissed off he or she's gonna be

if you touch that thing!"
A young guy
comes running over,
jumps onto the tracks
and lifts the lady up,
depositing her on the platform.
He holds her
waiting for the police,
who do get there pretty quickly.
My train finally arrives and I go home,
amazed at how the Universe works.

ABOUT THE AUTHOR

Ron Kolm is a contributing editor of *Sensitive Skin*. Ron is the author of *Divine Comedy*, *Duke & Jill*, *Suburban Ambush*, *Night Shift*, *A Change in the Weather*, *Welcome to the Barbecue* and *Swimming in the Shallow End*. He's had work in *Abwarts*, *And Then*, *The Café Review*, *Feuerstuhl*, *Gathering of the Tribes*, *Great Weather for Media*, *Live Mag!*, *Local Knowledge*, *Maintenant*, *NYC From the Inside*, *The Opiate*, the *Poets of Queens* anthology, *Public Illumination Magazine*, *The Red Wheelbarrow*, the *Riverside Poets Anthology*, *The Silver Tongued Devil Anthology*, *Sparring With Beatnik Ghosts Omnibus*, *Stadtgelichter* and the *Brownstone Poets* anthologies. Ron's papers were purchased by the New York University Library.

Made in the USA
Middletown, DE
18 August 2023

36711646R00056